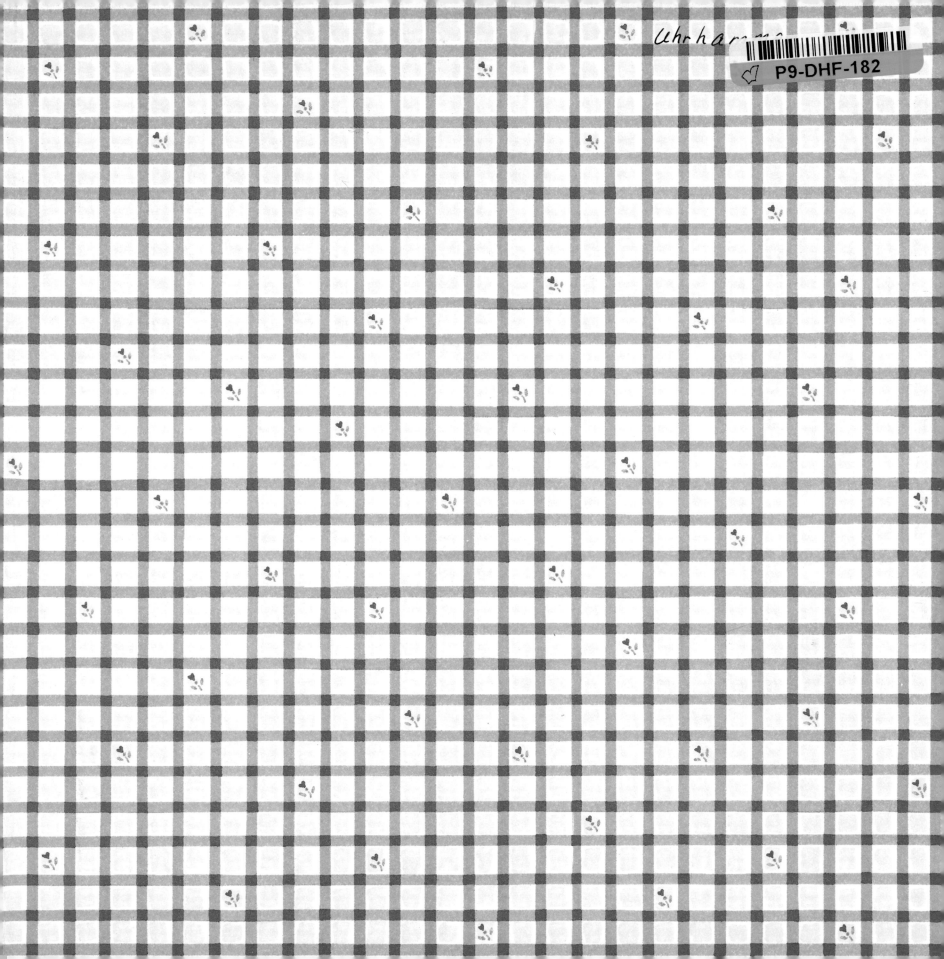

Mary Engelbreit's
Home Companion

Mary Engelbreit's
Home Companion

The Mary Engelbreit Look and How to Get It

Illustrations by Mary Engelbreit

Text by Charlotte Lyons

Photographs by Barbara Elliott Martin

Andrews and McMeel

A Universal Press Syndicate Company

Kansas City

is a registered trademark of Mary Engelbreit Enterprises, Inc.

10 9 8 7 6

ISBN: 0-8362-4621-7

Library of Congress Catalog Card Number: 94-070507

Text design by Stephanie Raaf

Contents

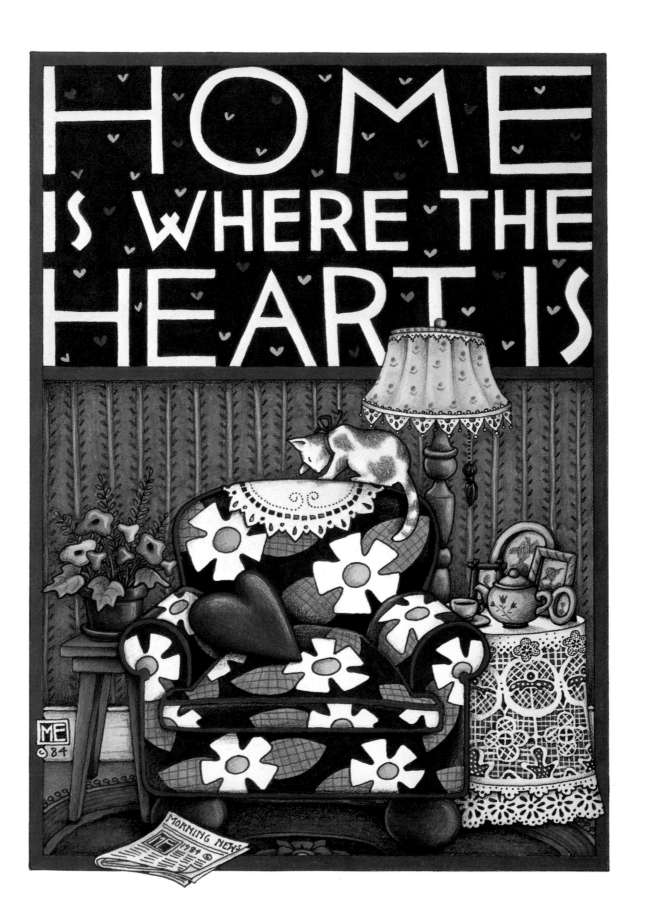

Introduction

I love houses. I love decorating houses. My husband, Phil, calls it "making a nest." Of course, he wishes I would just make the nest and be done with it, but that's not how I work. There's always a picture to be hung or a wonderful useless thing from a flea market to be jammed in someplace. I've had to hang pictures just to cover the nail holes left by other pictures that have been moved somewhere else! But that's the fun of decorating, I think—the possibilities are endless. Rearranging rooms, trying new colors, new styles—it keeps things interesting. And decorating is my way of relaxing after spending long, intense hours in my studio. And, best of all, there are no deadlines! I can take as long as I want to paint a chair or decorate a lamp and the end result is, I hope, still a cozy and welcoming place for my family and friends.

To imagine is everything!

I love to see how other people decorate their houses, too. It says so much about the people who live there. And, certainly, it gives you more wonderful ideas for your own house! My close friend Charlotte Lyons, who wrote the text for this book, has always been a great inspiration to me. We think alike and our houses are sisters in style, although each has the distinct imprint of the families who live there. When she leaves my house, she has new ideas percolating; after a visit to her house, I come back to mine with renewed interest and a burning desire to scramble everything up and start all over.

In this book, we don't show you anything that you'll need a decorator to reproduce. We believe the fun in making a house truly your own is in doing it yourself, using the things you love, making it comfortable for all the members of your family. What do you care if that strange bright green you love isn't "in" this year? It's your house and it should be filled with the things and the colors that make you feel good. Be inventive, be creative, make mistakes. Remember, there is very little that can't be painted over, slipcovered, camouflaged, or disguised as something else. Learn to see the decorative possibilities in unusual things—cans from the grocery store, twigs, berries and leaves from the garden, an empty picture frame in a corner of a junk store.

Through the eyes of our talented friend, photographer Barbara Elliott Martin, we have assembled our ideas about decorating. Using our houses and the homes of many other like-minded people, we hope to give you a lot of different approaches to "making your nest." Use our projects as they are or as jumping off points for your own ideas. Everyone starts somewhere—start with the place you love best.

-ME

Thinking is more interesting than knowing but not so interesting as looking.

For our husbands-
Phil, Andy and Bud

ENTRIES

"The beauty of the house is order,
The blessing of the house is contentment;
The glory of the house is hospitality."

-Anonymous

Whether you are coming home or greeting guests, your entry tells a story about your home. It presents a style that engages our attention and sets the tone for other rooms to follow. Relaxed or formal, the entry should offer the best invitation to continue. There should be room to drop mail and to hang up a jacket. In a house with children, a basket for mittens is useful as well as a mirror for last-minute hat checks. But, most of all, the entry should provide a welcoming transition from the outside world to the interior.

■ ■ ■ ■ ■ ■

Layers of lovely things
await attention here (opposite).
A lampshade embellished
with silk leaves
presides over a collection
of boxes and inkwells.
Beneath the table,
larger boxes and luggage
fill the space without
being in the way.
One large piece of art,
elegantly ornamented
with branches and flowers,
unifies the scene.

An assortment of collectibles gathers on a dropleaf table covered with a rag rug (below).
The printer's tray invites a closer look as does the charming collage of fruit labels
made for a Girl Scout project long ago.
This entry considers the point of view of children who come and go, too,
and love to have a mirror or artwork hung at their own height (left).

It is a long walk upstairs
to a third floor flat,
but the greeting is cheerfully given
by this antique hall tree (opposite).
Brimming with hats, umbrellas,
and accessories,
it offers a spot to kick off shoes
and shed the world's cares.

A diminutive secretary desk and delicate chair
fill this tiny entry with sophistication (below).
Art nouveau collectibles and a single piece of artwork
supply detail and warmth in a serene environment.

Beneath a gallery of family photos,
the front hall wall is simply decorated
with a few small frames
that draw attention
to the chest of drawers (above).
The intricately patterned wallpaper
ensures an intimate environment
that is relaxed and welcoming.

Watch Make It

Sunflower Mirror

Materials:
- A barnwood-style frame, 18" x 15"
- 3 silk sunflowers
- 8 twigs: four approximately 22" and four approximately 19"
- Mirror cut to fit inside frame dimensions
- Glazing points
- Cardboard to finish mirror
- Craft paper and double-stick tape to seal back of mirror
- Picture hanger
- Hot glue gun
- Silk butterfly accent

How **T**o:

After installing the mirror with glazing points and a putty knife, install a picture hanger on the back of the frame. Finish the back of the mirror with cardboard and protective paper, sealed with double-stick tape. (These picture-framing items can be bought at a craft store or at a do-it-yourself frame shop.)

Turn the framed mirror over to the front and lay out the twigs across the wood frame. When you have a pleasing or suitable arrangement, hot glue the twigs in place. Add the sunflowers across the top, clipping unnecessary stem lengths away, but allowing some stems to come down the front of the frame. Hot glue these into place. Accent a twig or flower with the butterfly and glue in place.

■ ■ ■ ■ ■ ■

"Whatever you can do,
or dream you can, begin it."

-Goethe

THE LOVE OF LEARNING, THE SEQUESTERED NOOKS, AND ALL THE SWEET SERENITY OF BOOKS

·LONGFELLOW·

"What I love is near at hand."

-Theodore Roethke

For those who collect—books or everything else—shelves are essential to enjoying the overall look of such things. Open shelves provide a vertical texture that keeps favorite treasures in view and, at the same time, they create interest on the wall.

When filling a shelf, experiment with different shapes and forms, mix in collectibles with books or small framed pictures, and use the back of the shelves to create depth. Treat each shelf as an integral part of the whole wall, but with its own focus and arrangement.

Cuphooks hung under the shelf or lacy trim attached to the shelf edges add more possibilities. Every now and then, take something out and add a new piece or group of books—it makes it all the more fun!

Although most shelves
are devoted to books,
many hold collectibles or
small drawings, too (opposite).
Each shelf welcomes inspection
when colorful covers
are displayed face-front.
Framed cards can be put to use
in the same way
to break up the background
of stored books.

If you have knowledge, let others light their candles by it.

An antique dishrack now features
a collection of ceramic dogs
and photo albums (below).
Over a chest of drawers,
this piece is an unusual addition
that dresses up a corner.
The dramatic pattern of the rug on the wall
unifies the two wall colors.

Colorful textiles and sculpture
layer the shelves of a rustic cupboard (above).
The birdhouse is irresistible
for more than one reason.

Cleverly put to use as a bookshelf
and side table,
this library ladder now stays put
in a living room corner (opposite).
The topiaries and lamp create different levels
to offset the books
and framed photographs.
Relaxed, yet focused,
the arrangement is engaging
without seeming fussy or overdone.

Gardening books among teapots and floral plates
make this built-in seem less single-minded (below).
Mixing china patterns and sizes succeeds
as long as the general feeling is muted.
Pretty napkins, folded open and used as shelf trim,
visually connect each shelf.

In a family room,
where a television set and stereo
take center-stage on a main wall,
the remaining space is filled
with treasures and old tins (above).
The dark frames and images
work with the black shapes
of speakers and the television screen
to soften the overall picture.

Watch Make It

Birdhouse Bookends

Materials:

- One pair standard bookends from the hardware store
- Two birdhouse fronts from the craft store
- Acrylic paints and brushes
- Glue

How To:

Paint both sides of the birdhouse fronts yellow. Paint the roof red and the base of the birdhouse green. Paint the perch white and then stripe the perch with black. Paint the bookend base green. Glue birdhouse to bookend base, keeping the back of the birdhouse centered and flush against the bookend stand.

■ ■ ■ ■ ■ ■

"I love everything that's old;
old friends, old times, old manners,
old books, old wines."

-Oliver Goldsmith

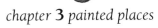

PAINTED PLACES

"You are looking as fresh as paint."

-Francis Smedley, 1850

Using paint as a decorating tool has become a popular and inexpensive pursuit. The limits are endless and the surfaces are surprising. Put it on the walls, the floors, the furniture and even fabric. Use it boldly and without worry because if you don't like the end results, you can paint over it!

With children, whose charming designs are often exceptional, use paint to transform an old piece of furniture into an heirloom. Duplicating a design from fabric or dishes is another safe way to begin on your own to explore the use of paint.

Above all, make it yours with the way you experiment in color and form. You may like your mistakes and want to repeat the same ones over and over in a pattern. This may result in your best look yet!

■ ■ ■ ■ ■ ■

A vaulted ceiling
at the top of the stairs
was painted to resemble
a starry night over
a fairy-tale village (opposite).
The chandelier
and heavy gilt moulding
further adorn the fantasy.

IT IS ART THAT MAKES LIFE, MAKES INTEREST, MAKES IMPORTANCE, AND I KNOW OF NO SUBSTITUTE FOR THE *FORCE* AND BEAUTY OF ITS PROCESS. HENRY JAMES

Given to her parents as a wedding gift,
Charlotte repainted this hutch
to use in her daughter's nursery (left).
Painted in the same style as Quimper dishes,
the drawers hold clothing and the shelves are currently outfitted
with nursery friends (below, left).
The new look, however,
would still be suitable back in the kitchen or den
where books would also fit the shelves.

Mary enhanced this bedroom bookcase
with a fisher-elf and his catch (above).
Drawn lightly in pencil and filled in with acrylics,
the whimsical treatment is a happy addition
to an otherwise plain wall.

This painted desk set
takes advantage of every
surface and detail (left).
Using mostly black and white,
with pink and green flowers,
the overall plan is playful,
but orderly.
Old books and china
bring a traditional feeling
to the exuberance
of paint and pattern.

After painting the floor uniformly white,
large squares were marked
and alternately sponged blue (below).
A wallpaper border was applied
to give the look of a rug.
Polyurethane protects it all underfoot.

Blocking out a portion of the chair back and seat
is one way to approach a painted piece (above).
Working only on those areas
keeps the project less daunting.
The gold arrow and flourishes provide the finishing touches.

Watch  Make It

Faux Leopard Chair

Materials:

- One chair with leather or vinyl seat
- Black and gold permanent markers
- Gold paint
- Tassels and cording

How To:

Using a permanent marker, begin at the edge of the chair seat and use small, irregular strokes up and down to form an outside ring for the leopard spot— no taller than an inch or so. Each spot should be different from the last.

Scatter these randomly over the seat and back. Fill the center of each spot with similar strokes of permanent gold, although these should be finer and closer together than the black.

Use gold paint to embellish bands of trim on the chair or to bring out other design aspects featured on your chair. Finish with gold cording and tassels.

■ ■ ■ ■ ■ ■

"That irregular and intimate quality of things
made entirely by the human hand."

-Willa Cather

KITCHENS

"No matter where I serve my guests,
it seems they like my kitchen best."

-Anonymous

Our kitchen is the heart of the home, the place where we come together for cooking, eating, meeting, and enjoying. Building an environment that can do all of these things efficiently is a challenge. This is the room that evolves over time, filling up with cherished pieces side by side with the newest gizmos.

Keeping the work surfaces free demands greater use of walls, inventive choices in accessories, and careful storage. Glass-front cabinets and cupboards allow pretty dishes to be seen. Collections and favorite patterns fill niches.

All of the following kitchens feature checkerboards as the dominant design motif—whether it appears in the tile, wallpaper, fabric, or paint. The timeless graphic both warms and enlivens each space.

■ ■ ■ ■ ■ ■

Soothing country colors
dapple the walls
and call for an eclectic
assortment of baskets,
botanicals, and dishes (opposite).
The colors of fruits
and vegetables
mix naturally here
where informality is the intent.

Indigo blue-and-white checkers
direct attention to an efficient, yet charming workspace
where fiesta ware contributes colorful flavor
to glass-front cabinets (below).
Folk-art styles mix happily with the homey shades
of red and yellow against the blue and white.

Charlotte painted tiles with an overglaze
and had them refired for permanence (above).
Enclosed in a checkered frame,
the tile mural impacts the space, is easy to clean,
and reminds everyone that cooking should be a pleasure,
not a chore.
Restaurant-style burners and butcher block countertops
assist each other to make the most of a small niche
where everything is quickly within reach.

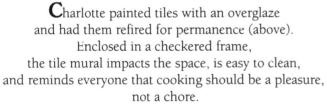

Mary's kitchen is chock-full of cherries and checkers.
A Welsh dresser holds teapots
as well as her hand-painted china pieces on top (opposite).
Cherries brighten the painted floor
and most of the serving pieces in the cupboards.
Filled to capacity with cheerfulness,
this is a delightful place to enjoy food with family or friends.

Small checkerboards emphasize the larger one
in a room where cabinet doors and window mullions
echo the pattern as well (below).
A few collectible finds kept above the workspace create playfulness
without interfering with the business of cooking (above).

Reminiscent of a diner,
checkerboards guarantee a lively look
and simple white cabinets eliminate
the need for clutter in the kitchen (above).
Red accents spot the room with warmth and contrasting appeal.
Black and white are easy colors to work with
because the standard shades
are consistently reproduced everywhere.

Watch  **Make It**

Hand-Painted Cannisters

Materials:
- One set of white ceramic cannisters
- Liquitex Glossies paints in assorted colors
- Brushes

How **T**o:
Using a water-based marker, transfer your design onto the fronts of the cannisters. Paint in large shapes first, then add outlines and vines. Bake according to product instructions.

■ ■ ■ ■ ■ ■

"One's home is the safest refuge to everyone."

-Sir Edward Coke

TO KNOW IS NOTHING AT ALL; TO IMAGINE IS EVERYTHING.

ANATOLE FRANCE THIBAULT

WINDOWS

"Remember, it's impossible to sit by a window that you won't want to keep."

-John Heard

The windows in our rooms are the sources of light, air, and daydreams. Since they are such a large part of the room's design, windows call for a lot of imagination in the way we dress them. Unless privacy is an issue, simple, open treatments are best. Use the sills as shelves to connect the glass to the room and create another place to show off the things we love. The top of the window is our favorite place to decorate, whether it's done with a valance of wood or with fabric. Like a fanciful hat, a window treatment shouldn't obstruct the view, but, rather, add to the loveliness.

■ ■ ■ ■ ■ ■

Three fabrics are wrapped and stapled from a central knot to fashion an elaborate swag over a bedspread split and hung as curtains (opposite). In a cottage living room, this is both elegant and casual. The dark wicker and bookcases complement the easy style of weekend comfort.

Magical antlers weave a crown
above primitive iron silhouettes
on this large central window (opposite).
The delicate cutouts cast lacy shadows
on sunny days or starry nights without obstructing the view.

Do you have a pretty tablecloth like this one (above)?
Drape it over a spring rod to dress up plain sheers.
Mary painted the blue and white console to pick up
the polka dots and stripes that seem to be everywhere.
Staying with one main color scheme
of mostly blue and white makes it work.

A tiny architectural window holds
an intimate arrangement of collectible favorites (above).
Beneath it a simple accordion rack
provides a changing drapery of coats and hats.

In a small master bath this tiled window sill
doubles as a dressing table (below).
The twig and decoupaged screen anchors the vignette
and repeats the pretty gothic window shapes and trees outside.
Simple sheers stretched on tension rods
are subtle window treatments that work almost anywhere.
The upper sills provide extra shelves for vintage bath accessories.

Mary transferred a favorite design
to wooden valances presiding over crisp eyelet panels
from the department store (above).
The tops display collectibles
and little treasures in a playful parade.

Watch  Make It

Canvas Valance

Materials:

- Artist's canvas
- Scissors
- Measuring tape
- Glue
- Acrylic paints and brushes
- Thumbtacks or staple gun

How To:

Measure window from moulding to moulding width at the wall. Add 1" to this measurement. Cut a strip of canvas 15" by this adjusted measurement. To find the center, fold the strip in half. Keeping it folded, and cutting through both thicknesses, mark and cut away two triangles, leaving 1" at the side edges. The top of each triangle should be 5" from the bottom edge.

Clip the top of each triangle 1/2" and fold up the raw edges. Press and glue the hem. Also press and glue the side hems. Using a pencil, transfer the paint pattern to the triangle points and top edge.

Paint the design onto the canvas, allowing it to dry thoroughly between colors. When completely dry, staple or tack to the top of the moulding and at the sides near the top also. Dry clean only.

"I remember, I remember
The house where I was born,
The little window where the sun
Came peeping in at morn."

-Thomas Hood, 1827

*chapter **6** fireplaces*

BE WARM, INSIDE & OUT.

• 49 •

FIREPLACES

"Be warm-inside and out."

Naturally the center of attention, a fireplace offers a place to gather in every room. A strong piece of artwork, the best collectibles, and fresh flowers whenever possible belong here. Comfortable chairs and baskets of reading material are welcome ingredients as are pillows, moveable tables, and games.

For the holidays, repopulate the mantel with seasonal collectibles or boast a new treasure where everyone will see it. Collections easily convene on the mantel shelf as well. This is the spot to focus on "favorites."

■ ■ ■ ■ ■ ■

One beautiful painting
by artist Terry Moeller
reigns over this living room
hearth where mantel accents
are quiet, yet sophisticated,
in porcelain and silver (opposite).
The dark wall color
focuses attention on the richness
of fresh flowers and crystal
sparkling in the firelight.

Flanked by silhouettes
of Mom and Dad,
this elaborate mantel
chosen from a salvage yard
is a showcase for
assorted collectibles (left).
The hand-colored
paper doll cut out is a quick
project as is the child's chair
sweetened with checkers
and bright bands of colors.

Checkerboards come in pink and white, too,
as shown in this sunny fireplace at the beach (below).
A framed print of children at the seashore
and some favorite china balance the eucalyptus
in an old water pitcher.
The green cabinet beside the fire anchors
a small picture grouping
of antique postcards in delicate frames.
Old wicker chairs are light enough to scoot closer
for warmth after a cool evening stroll.

A bedroom fireplace is a delicious luxury
in a getaway where "fairy tales do come true" (above).
Marbleized in soft shades of peach and yellow,
the hearth changes seasons
with seashells and potted amaryllis.
A chaise draws near—
the perfect choice for reading or resting.

"**A** chair of bowlies" warms the spring hearth
in this dining room (left).
The pretty oak and beveled mirror mantel
boasts the best of a collection
of ceramic platters and teacups.
All the colors reappear on the table
where a vintage tablecloth ties everything together.

A fireplace made from massive river rocks
inspires the combination of rustic furnishings (above).
Quilts, birdhouses, and a primitive screen
are natural accents.

Watch Make It

Fire Screen

Materials:

- 3 solid-panel shutters, approximately 12" by 25"
- 4 sets of hinges and tools to install them
- 3 wooden legs
- Decorative wood moulding, cut to the length of the top edges of the shutters
- Glue
- Acrylic paints and brushes
- Acrylic sealer and brush

How To:

Hinge the shutter panels together to fold in a "U-shape." Attach the legs to the base. Paint a base color on the front and back, using a dark paint such as black or navy. Transfer the main design onto the center panel, using a white pencil. Fill in the shapes with acrylic decorative paints. Repeat, using simple designs on the side panels and accent pieces. Paint the wood trim before attaching it to the top. Glue the finished trim to the top edge. Seal all surfaces on the front with acrylic sealer.

"The happiest moments of my life
have been the few which I have passed at home
in the bosom of my family."

-Thomas Jefferson

COZY CORNERS

"Friends, books, a cheerful heart and conscience clear
are the most choice companions we have here."

William Mather

The intent of any home should be physical comfort. Having places to recline and relax are essential. Big chairs, cozy window seats, and deeply luxurious chaises offer the moments of reflection when we can enjoy our efforts.

An inviting corner may contain many things or just a few, but the basics should include a table for books, a pillow or two for support, and a good light for reading. Whenever possible, room should be made for two. Conversation is an element that can be supplied only by a friend.

■ ■ ■ ■ ■ ■

Children have room
to spread seashells
among the sunlit patches
on this porch (opposite).
Pull-up rockers and eclectic
pillows are just right
for reading or conversation.
The best shells line up on the rail
to begin a collection.
For extra comfort,
a throw rug in beach stripes
comes up easily for weather
changes or sandy clean-up.

Elegantly suited to a living room corner,
this screen encloses a lovely chair and expansive
ottoman (opposite).
Faux leopard and needlepoint
are sophisticated complements
to the luggage used here as a table.
The standing lamp casts a tall,
broad light and leaves the table free
for books or a glass.

In the sitting room off a master bedroom,
a sumptuous chair beckons a visitor (below).
Crowned with favorite photographs,
a soft pillow, and a decoupaged footstool,
it's an excellent place for retreat
before or after a long day.
The dressmaker's form now holds
a fanciful array of dress-up pins.

In Mary's family room,
this overstuffed chair is the envy of anyone who didn't get there first (above).
The wainscoting creates visual interest
while deep cushions combine with magazine racks and low tables
to offer every other comfort.
A collection of wooden boxes fills one side table.
These emphasize the mixture of patterns used in the fabrics as well.

Everyone needs a place to hide away now and then (above).
This bedroom window seat is the ideal spot with its wide view of the yard,
lots of pillows, and room to stretch out.
Keeping the pillows neutral allows many to bank together.
The tray table can be easily moved to any spot.

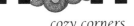

Watch Make It

Decoupage Lampshade

Materials:
- One black paper lampshade
- Paper with cherry-pattern repeat (stationery, gift wrap, or wallpaper)
- X-acto knife
- Glue stick, Spray Mount™, or thin, white glue
- Acrylic sealer

How **T**o:

Cut out cherries from the pattern with an X-acto knife. Position them on the lampshade in a desirable pattern. Glue into place, carefully wiping away excess glue and smoothing edges. When complete, seal all over with the acrylic sealer. Do not over apply the sealer—this will cause the paper shade to buckle. Dry thoroughly.

"I love it—I love it.
Who shall dare
to chide me for loving
that old arm chair?"

-Eliza Cook

PILLOWS

"Leisure for reverie, gay or somber,
does much to enrich life."

-Miriam Beard

Like candies in a box, pillows are meant to be rich and luscious. Masses of them heaped onto a bed, or just a few tailored cushions on a sofa, make a room all the more inviting. The look of a room can be changed dramatically by alternating seasonal covers. Look for vintage embroideries, unfinished needlepoint, or beautiful patterns in fabrics. Made from remnants, tapestry, or perhaps your own needlework, pillows are a fast, easy, inexpensive way to cozy up a room.

■ ■ ■ ■ ■ ■

For Mary's birthday, Charlotte hooked this portrait pillow of her two sons (opposite). Piped in vivid red and backed in black and white gingham check, it echoes the children at play in the artwork above.

Thou shalt sit on a Cushion
And sew a fine seam
And feed upon Strawberries,
Sugar and Cream.

Chosen for their color and interest,
old textiles outfit new pillows (opposite).
Fancy fringes and embroidery can be found
at flea markets and estate sales.
Together with newer department store pillows,
they mix on a wicker chaise,
creating a feeling that is old-fashioned and comfy.

Taken from a Victorian calling card,
this phrase and image transfer beautifully
to a pillow top hooked from thin strips of wool (below).
Similar to needlepoint,
the finished work accentuates a sweet living room corner.

A band of tapestry combines with brocade
to create a sophisticated pillow (above).
The smaller round cushion employs pattern again as a companion,
this time using a different color.
The pair evokes a tranquil mood
when placed on the luxuriously appointed sleigh bed.

Brilliantly colored wool scraps are blanket-stitched into a traditional design
to celebrate a wedding (above).
Red wool, felted and cut into a zigzag pattern,
replaces a ruffle and adds to the graphic strength of the design.

Watch Make It

Tea Towel Pillow

Materials:
- One tea towel with decorative work or design
- Fabric backing
- Pillow cording covered in contrasting fabric
- Polyester stuffing
- Sewing machine
- Scissors
- Thread

How **T**o:

Two methods are given here:

Examine the towel to identify the best use of the design. If the towel does not have any stains, the remaining towel area can be used for the pillow back.

Use a straight edge and mark out the pillow dimensions carefully, keeping the design centered. Add seam allowances of 3/8" on all four sides. Mark and cut with scissors.

Use the front piece as your pattern and cut out a piece for the backing to the same size. For the back, either use the remaining towel or choose from a coordinating fabric.

Sandwich the two pieces, plus the pillow cording, right sides together. Pin all thicknesses together carefully to keep raw edges even. Machine-stitch

through all layers, leaving a 3" opening at the bottom. Turn right side out, stuff firmly with polyester stuffing, and hand-stitch the opening closed.

An alternative method of construction uses the entire towel. Fold the towel in half, right sides together, and adjust fold to desired dimensions for pillow. Machine-stitch across the towel. Cut away excess towel. Turn right side out. Center design. Top-stitch along one edge so that the towel-side edge becomes a decorative edge for the pillow. Stuff and stitch remaining side in the same way.

■ ■ ■ ■ ■ ■

"What is more agreeable than one's home?"

-Cicero

WALLS & PICTURES

"Have nothing in your house that you do not know to be useful, or believe to be beautiful."

-William Morris

Making a room pleasant to be in means infusing it with personality. The walls are a natural place to start. Whether they're vast and open or small and enclosed, they are begging for decoration. Hanging several frames in a group calls for a common denominator such as color, shape, or content. Sometimes a single piece will leave room for later additions.

Small shelves or a plate rail can become part of a wall arrangement, where plates and art can hang side by side. Take advantage of dishes that can be hung and use pedestals to display collectibles. Pretty ribbons can be used to accent frames or try silk flowers and postcards. Textiles such as quilts, rugs, and antique clothing are showcased in this manner also.

Four exquisite panels of an old nursery frieze intensify the importance of this corner (opposite). Set behind a table of beautiful objects, they are illuminated by the tall table lamp reflecting interest upward to the wall. The faded loveliness of each element expresses the serenity of the room.

Old smoker's tables congregate before a primitive chest,
supporting the fabulous clock house made by a retired metalsmith (above).
The geometric rug provides an exciting background
that adds the strength of a big piece to unify the other elements.

A weathered magazine table
is the base for this wall treatment
where each frame and shelf links the next (below).
The consistent use of red and black simplifies the look.
Experiment with little frame toppers and postcards
stuck here and there.

Purchased as a folio,
these prints fill a long wall with symmetry and detail (opposite).
Inexpensive wood frames were painted red, then gold-leafed.
In a room of understated richness,
they are simple and fresh.

Vintage travel postcards are enclosed in quick frames
for a rotating gallery of graphics (below).
Accompanied by old tin cars and an island lamp,
the rattan chair completes a theme corner
in this collector's home.

Hats, chairs and sentimental toys
work together to dress a wall
with imaginative fun (above).

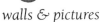

Watch Make It

Hand-Painted Frame

Materials:
- New or old wood picture frame with at least a 2" frame
- Acrylic paints and brushes
- Acrylic sealer

How **T**o:

Base-paint the picture frame in black. Using decorative paint colors, begin in one corner and paint the largest flowers first. Repeat that in the opposite corner. Switching back and forth, add new flower patterns to build the design down the frame sides. Add leaves and vines, polka dots and checkers as you wish. The look should be symmetrical, but not exactly so. Protect the frame with acrylic sealer. For a quick finish, use fabric as a self-mat with a photograph or greeting card on top. Complete the frame closure and hang.

"It takes a heap o' livin'
in a house t' make it home."

-Edgar Albert Guest

EVERYONE NEEDS THEIR OWN SPOT.

· ROBERT WHALEN ·

ODD SPOTS

"The greatest pleasure in life
is doing what people say you cannot do."

-Walter Bagehot

We are all challenged by small spaces that defy "the plan." They are nonetheless charming quirks that invite attention. Sometimes it is easy to know what to do—as in the case of a landing or thin wall where more pictures will do the trick.

Small vignettes often fill an awkward space—a hall devoted to costume jewelry and containers or a corner given to old toys and books. A few odd spots, however, are truly transformed into favorites with imagination and flair. We cherish all the opportunities for decorating our homes and delight in the discovery of new ideas for each.

Charlotte found this damaged, hooked rug at an estate sale and had it cut into strips, the raw edges serged, and installed as a runner (opposite). Now it leads a vintage path to older family photos, mixed with cross-stitched mottoes and textiles, completing a portrait of another generation.

This small landing allows room for a shallow cabinet big enough to boast a collection of lusterware (left). Mary combined the painted sisal mat and old Middle Eastern drape, unusual accessories that create interest without clutter. Lamplight is always preferable to overhead lighting and adds to the cozy feeling here.

A pie stand offers vertical storage
in a tight kitchen corner (below).

A narrow wall showcases an antique clock,
small frames, and a crystal decanter collection (above).
Each enhances the delicate nature of the others,
while making an elegant combination.

A small bathroom closet with the door removed
becomes a dramatic dressing area
with shelves created from plywood (below).
Trimmed out with new moulding and painted black inside,
some compartments stow cigar boxes of jewelry or make-up,
while others mix toiletries with collections.
This ingenious solution
would work in a kitchen or bedroom as well.

On the way down a steep stair,
a collection of old felt pennants revolves in a vibrant pinwheel
of college nostalgia (above).
Postcards and vintage luggage
populate the ledge with related memorabilia.

Watch [MI] Make It

Paper Cut-Out Border

Materials:
- Heavy paper for templates
- Colored copy or fade-proof paper
- Small, sharp paper scissors
- Teacher's putty or glue stick

How **T**o:

Transfer the pattern you have chosen to heavy paper for use as a template. Cut out one of each style. Begin with the base of the house. Trace template onto colored paper. Repeat for the number of houses needed. Cut out the patterns with scissors. Cut out the roof styles from contrasting colored paper.

Assemble the roof and house with the glue stick. Add small rectangles of roof color for windows and doors—or cut the doors out from the house. Repeat the same procedure for tree shapes.

Alternate houses and trees along straight edge of wall tile or border. Fasten to wall with small dabs of teacher's putty or glue. Cut out random grass shapes and lay them over the house and tree bases. Fasten in place. For a permanent design, these patterns should be transferred with paint to the wall.

"Where we love is home.
Home that our feet may leave
but not our hearts."

-Oliver Wendell Holmes

CHILDREN'S ROOMS

"Tall oaks from little acorns grow."

-Anonymous

Children love beautiful things as much as we do. Their imaginations are inspired by detail, color, and design. Nostalgia and sturdy antiques are excellent partners in children's rooms, as long as they indulge the pursuits of a child. Lots of comfortable storage, whether in baskets or cupboards, can manage the toys—although many toys can easily become part of the scheme when they're clustered in collections of their own.

Avoiding the conventional "cute" is easily accomplished with versatile furniture and appealing accents that can be changed to reflect the child's interests. With a solid base to work from, the various stages of childhood can evolve through the use of accessories. An alphabet quilt hung on the wall can be replaced with a whimsical theater poster for an older child. Let your children participate in this—you may be surprised by their good taste!

■ ■ ■ ■ ■ ■

Mary found this adorable nursery set just in time for a friend's new baby (opposite). Her hand-painted table and chairs look right at home here on the floor painted in a similar design. Putting the wallpaper border at eye level reduces the scale to a comfy child-height.

• 91 •

Repainting an older twin bed with checkers and gold leaf
launches a fantasy in this boy's room.
Yard sale suitcases, a gypsy tambourine, and lederhosen
complement the playfulness (opposite).
A calendar of Native American portraits
is an inexpensive way to transfer art to the walls.
To carry this scheme through the years,
the cocoa walls and sisal mat are neutral backdrops
that could support any style.

A glorious iron bed sparkles
in this bedroom fit for a princess (above).
Decidedly feminine but not fussy,
the basics are grown-up to avoid a remake later.
Accessories tell the story of a little girl now.
The fanciful armoire accommodates toys and books,
side by side with room to grow.

These former nursery walls now resemble a western sky
when the punch of black and white with desert colors
comes into the picture (above).
A classic bed and a card table used as a desk
make this a comfortable space
for a child and friends.

When this den had to become a girl's room,
Charlotte softened the dark walls with old toys, a bright quilt, and vintage pillows (above).
Vivid images pop out against the bottle green.
Cafe curtains add more crispness while the family portrait on a hooked rug
and the picket-fence bookshelf address the old-fashioned theme.
A plain red lamp takes white polka dots for a quick change.

Watch Make It

Bunny Lamp

Materials:

- Papier-mâché rabbit from the craft store
- Lamp base large enough for the rabbit to sit on
- Lamp kit and shade from the craft or hardware store
- Acrylic paints and brushes
- Acrylic sealer
- Glue

How To:

Referring to the photograph here, paint the papier-mâché rabbit with acrylic decorative paints. Paint the lamp base to coordinate. Embellish the base with decorations, if desired. Seal rabbit and lamp base with acrylic sealer. With a pencil, mark out the placement of the rabbit on the base. Remove rabbit and assemble lamp kit according to instructions. Reposition the rabbit and glue into place. Assemble with shade when completely dry.

**"One of the luckiest things that can happen to you in life is,
I think, to have a happy childhood."**

-Agatha Christie

"I would rather have roses on my table
than diamonds on my neck."

-Emma Goldman

Whether setting a table for a meal, or for a collection, careful thought should be given to detail and composition. A table is much like a large tray—an enclosed space for things. The ambience of a room or occasion is established here with pretty dishes, collectibles, and flowers. Mixing patterns and linens works for formal dinners as well as for casual entertaining. So, too, a collection of rocks from a river bed enhances a living room marble-topped table. Whatever you put out on your tables, it will be touched, admired, and questioned—so a tabletop's character and charm are everything.

■ ■ ■ ■ ■ ■

Anyone would be happy
to find breakfast waiting here
on this cheerful table set with
color and vitality (opposite).
The graphic sunflowers
and checkers are well-suited
to the rich red chairs.
In a white room
with an expansive garden window,
this is clearly the indoor focus.
A child's artwork
enlivens the scene.

Grandmother's dining room set dresses up or down
with baskets beside porcelain,
a gilt mirror beside a postcard collection,
and a tattered quilt beneath wedding china (below).
Combining elegance with everyday color and texture
makes the room usable at all times.

These bronze cherubs
float a glass tabletop above their wings (above).
Favorite pieces of crystal gather here with other collectibles
on a table that commands great attention on its own.

A mix-and-match table is set with odd pieces of china
and inexpensive basics (opposite).
Layering green and pink patterns
with white brings it all together in a kitchen corner
softened with lace panels and a few seaside favorites.

Rustic elegance takes this table out of the ordinary
where personal things mingle
with found treasures and favorite objects (below).
Treating each piece as a sculpture of different height and form
creates a still life of changing interest.

Lovely books stacked on a central table
create pedestals for cherished objects (above).
The crystal and quills make the foreground delicately fascinating
while the statue works in the same way
that a lamp might to build height.

Watch ME Make It

Papier-mâché Bowls

Materials:

- Newspaper shredded in 1"-2" strips
- Bowl used for form, covered in foil
- Paste made from 1 cup water, 1/2 cup flour, 1 tablespoon white glue
- Acrylic paints and brushes
- Acrylic sealer
- Pieces of raffia, ribbon, or twigs

How To:

Wrap the outside of a bowl shape with foil. Mix paste and dip strips of newspaper into paste. Remove excess paste and lay on the foil, strip by strip. Placement of strips should at first resemble the spokes of a basket forming an "X" over the bottom. Later, the strips may run around the width of the bowl. The first layer should cover all the foil, but not too thickly. Do not wrap the strips over the top rim of the bowl or on the inside. Allow to dry overnight.

When thoroughly dry, apply another layer. This time, add trim pieces and layer over them with newspaper strips.

Again, dry overnight. Repeat for another layer and dry overnight.

After the third layer is dry, carefully remove the foil from the bowl. Then pull the foil gently away from the paper bowl. Sand lightly. Paint the base of the bowl with white paint, inside and out. Base-paint again with a color.

When dry, decorate with patterns that use repeat designs. Try a different pattern on the inside. Seal with acrylic sealer when complete. These are decorative containers and are unsuitable for liquids or food.

"Nothing good was ever
achieved without enthusiasm."

-Ralph Waldo Emerson

COLLECTIONS

"Give me the luxuries of life and I will do without the necessities."

-Frank Lloyd Wright

A collection isn't born overnight. One treasure on a tabletop is soon accompanied by one more, and so on. This gradual building of a collection ensures the fun that comes from seeking new additions. Weeding out and replacing pieces with new favorites keeps the collector at work. Displaying these things is the creative challenge.

For whatever reason you've chosen your collections, display them fondly and lovingly. Any surface is suitable for a collection—in a cupboard, on a wall, in a tray, on a window sill—as long as the connection of one to another is clear. For example, small things need close proximity; large things can punctuate a room. Also, consider that providing a subtle counterpoint to a collection is refreshing and adds relief, such as mixing a hen among a field of roosters.

Collecting the things that appeal to you increases their appeal to others. Beware—this passion takes on a life of its own! We wonder if there are any limits to the art.

■ ■ ■ ■ ■ ■

Old dolls represent only one collection
of many shown here (opposite).
Weather-telling houses, sheep and chickens
ornament a living room hutch
tucked into an alcove.
The Noah's Ark and picture books
establish a theme of childhood memories
and charm.

In this formal dining room,
a collection of baby dishes in a mirrored cabinet
is a surprise to those who expect heirloom china (below).
The dark green walls and children's portraits
also diminish the formality,
adding an intimacy that welcomes children and dinner guests alike.

Carefully chosen for their history and craft,
antique baskets spill forth from a rustic cupboard (below).
Baskets are easily collected and wonderfully pleasing
en masse or alone.
The added storage is an extra advantage.
Usefulness makes any collection more valuable.

Myriad shapes and sizes of scotty dogs
romp across this dresser top (opposite).
Handmade valentine collages by the owner, Linda Solovic,
along with family photos designate this a best-loved vignette.
"Spot, the Cat" watches warily as though looking through a window.

Vintage brides and grooms fill a tabletop shelf with happy memories and starstruck glances (above).
In the home of newlyweds, they are a romantic tribute to their newfound happiness.

collections

Watch Make It

Valentine Tray

Materials:

- One wooden tray with handles and a rim around the edge
- Glass cut to fit the inside area
- Decorative ribbon trim
- Fabric or wrapping paper large enough to fit inside
- Assortment of old valentines or other paper collections
- Acrylic paints and brushes
- Glue or Spray Mount™

How To:

Paint the tray in a favorite color to contrast with interior. Use a blank piece of scrap paper and press it inside the tray opening. Use a pencil to crease the edges of the scrap paper to create an exact pattern. Remove and use as a pattern to cut your actual design. Use this same pattern to have the glass cut so that the fit will be snug.

Lightly glue lining paper to the interior of the tray. Use ribbon or trim to border paper, if desired, and glue in place. Arrange valentines on top of

paper lining. Use the smallest amount of glue to tack into place. Clean the glass and place it gently over design. Do not glue it down so that the collection can be rotated and the glass can be removed for cleaning.

• 111 •

**"Beauty is everlasting and
dust is for a time."**

-Marianne Moore

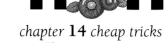

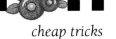

CHEAP TRICKS

"Use it up, wear it out;
Make it do, or do without."

-New England Proverb

To imagine a project, master it quickly, and have it done in a wink is unusually satisfying. Because we like quick results, these simple projects are what we call "cheap tricks." Using old objects in new ways, recycling others, or just faking a new look is a great pleasure. They don't have to be "forever" changes, but often they inspire others that are. Invent your own cheap tricks with ingenuity and change the looks of your home instantly for next to nothing.

■ ■ ■ ■ ■ ■

These graphic labels
are too cute to stash
in a cupboard (opposite).
Found at an Italian
specialty food shop,
they double as flower holders
when empty.
At fifty cents apiece,
they are a great value
for decorating or dinner!

Common shelving brackets and standards are cleverly disguised with fabric and collections (above).
The blue and white scheme blends all together, but welcomes the touch of color given by a tulip or book cover.
When assembling dishes in a group, slightly damaged or chipped pieces
are inexpensive to collect and don't show their flaws as readily.

In a tight spot near the front door
a small coat rack made from an unfinished peg board
encourages the children to hang up their things (below).
Covered with an allover painted pattern,
it was a snap to make and install.
Charlotte made the felt jacket for her daughter,
taking full advantage of the scrap box, old buttons,
and a child's imagination.

Raggedy Ann and Andy dolls
rest under a vintage handkerchief
tacked in a tiny window (above).
Several are used in this way
to warm little bedroom windows
that double as shelves for small toys.
The cherry glass ornament
completes the vignette sweetly.

Charlotte's husband
built the READ box to use
for housing magazines and catalogs,
but an interesting box
of any sort would do the same job
repainted and mounted
on the wall (left).
An old stepstool took new paint, too,
with sponge-painted checkers
and quick brush strokes.

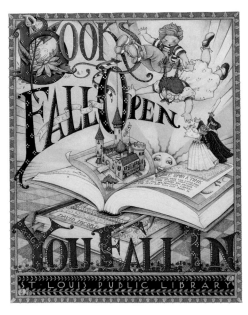

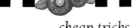
Watch Make It

Framed Papercutting

Materials:

- Secondhand frame
- Typing paper
- Backing paper in a dark color
- Small scissors
- Spray Mount™ or glue stick

How To:

Place the frame over the typing paper and trace the inside opening. Choose a design like this one that takes advantage of the interior frame space. Fold the typing paper in half and pencil one half of the design. With the paper folded, use the scissors to carefully cut through both layers so that the design is mirrored when opened. Cut away large areas first, then smaller ones. Open and mount on backing paper that has been cut to fit the frame. Finish frame closure and hang.

■ ■ ■ ■ ■ ■

"The highest form of bliss is living with
a certain degree of folly."

-Erasmus

WORKSPACES

"Imagination is more important than knowledge."

-Einstein

Once a village firehouse, Mary's studio sprawls across the second floor of the firefighters' former dormitory. Although the room looks dramatically different now, it still offers a call to action. Surrounded by the images of fantasy, delight, and wonder, Mary has built an environment that engages her creative spirit from start to finish.

There is a place to relax while reading, a spacious drawing table with everything near at hand, and excellent storage areas for reference books and completed works. But, of course, the greatest element is the room-sized bulletin-board effect that offers inspiration at every turn.

■ ■ ■ ■ ■ ■

Uninterrupted quiet
is a mandate issued by
Mary's playful sign (opposite).
A panoramic view
highlights the drawing table
at right where Mary spends
long hours at work.

THE REAL VOYAGE OF DISCOVERY CONSISTS NOT IN SEEKING NEW LANDSCAPES BUT IN HAVING NEW EYES.

MARCEL PROUST

Between a flat file case and layout table,
this niche beneath the window is outfitted
with one of Mary's characters cut from plywood (below).
Her tabletop tray offers a bowl of—what else?—cherries.

Vivid pattern and rich color
mix throughout the studio (above).
Casual furniture provides a spot for Mary's sons
to gather here and review their mother's work in progress.
ME licensed dolls gather on a shelf
where they can watch, too.

Christmas cards are drawn in July
and this little feather tree and snowmen friends
do their best to generate seasonal spirit (above).
Charlotte's papercut angel hovers over a mirrored shelf
that Mary revived with style and charm.

Sunlight illuminates small toys
and trinkets sparkling with whimsy (above).
Books for reference are neatly shelved beneath a counter
holding extra pencils and markers.

Watch MF Make It

Portfolio

Materials:

- Artist's portfolio 10" x 12" available at an art supply store
- Decorative gift wrap paper in two contrasting patterns
- Wooden beads
- Decorative ribbon or trim
- Decorative label
- Acrylic paints and brushes
- Glue stick or Spray Mount™
- Scissors
- Acrylic sealer

How To:

Use one pattern of the gift wrap for the outside. Cut one strip, 15" x 4-1/2". Cut four other rectangles, 4" x 7". Place rectangles across each of the outside four corners, front and back. Wrap excess paper to inside. Trim, remove, and glue. Replace and smooth wrinkles. Allow to dry. Glue long strip. With portfolio open, place on spine. Wrap over top and bottom edge to inside. Close portfolio to ease the pressure and adjust the cover. Reopen

and allow to dry. Cover cut edges of paper on the outside with ribbon. Wrap onto inside in the same way as the paper. If desired, add a decorative label to the front cover and print a name or title of contents. Line the inside with contrasting paper to within 1/4" of edges. Slip beads onto ribbon

ties. Tie knots above and below beads to hold in place. Paint dots randomly on front and back cover. Seal outside work and paper with acrylic sealer. Dry thoroughly.

■ ■ ■ ■ ■ ■

Credits

■ ■ ■ ■

Grateful appreciation to the homes of:

Ann Marie and Steve Allen
Webster Groves, Missouri
pages 39, 114

Kate and Ken Anderson
St. Louis, Missouri
page 21, 77

Robin Winge and Michael Dinges
Oak Park, Illinois
pages 69, 76, 86, 102

Jim Whiteley and Karen Foss
University City, Missouri
pages 14, 26, 31, 38, 44, 46, 60, 61, 68, 87, 98, 110

Gregory and Susanne Hoffman
St. Louis, Missouri
page 38

Diane and Bob Josephs
Houston, Texas
pages 20, 34, 78, 85, 92, 102

Linda Solovic and Gary Karpinski
St. Louis, Missouri
pages 54, 78, 109

Maggie Montray
St. Louis, Missouri
page 90

Nan and John Morris
Oak Park, Illinois
page 37

Jeff and Anne O'Connor
Oak Park, Illinois
page 93

Steve and Susan Smith
Kirkwood, Missouri
page 53

Jill and David Stewart
Oak Park, Illinois
page 54

Deborah and Dan Taylor
Webster Groves, Missouri
pages 22, 86

Donn Warden
Alton, Illinois
pages 10, 12, 21, 30, 45, 85, 116

Sonja and Robert Willman
St. Louis, Missouri
pages 42, 55, 69, 71

Special thanks to Monsanto and Wear-Dated carpet

Contributing designers:

John Hunn
St. Louis, Missouri
page 26

Peg Patton for Daisy Kingdom
page 29

Chp Trx
St. Louis, Missouri
pages 36, 46, 90

Special thanks to Jean Lowe, Stephanie Raaf, Stephanie Barken, and Ray Kersting.